Contents

What is a game changer?

Game changers are people who use their skills, talents and ideas to change the world! They sometimes have to fight to be allowed to do what they believe in, but they never give up.

The hidden heroes

Imagine you did something amazing, but someone else got the praise. Or even worse, nobody noticed what you had done at all! You would probably feel terrible.

Well, that is what happened to the people in this book. It is time to put things right and give them credit where it is due!

Spectacular scientists

Scientists help us to learn how the world works. Many also often work out how to make the world better!

Lise Meitner

The scientists in this section have come up with brilliant ways of understanding and improving our world. So why didn't they get the credit for what they had done?

Alice Ball

Perhaps it is because they were all women at a time when men were in charge. However, despite all this, they still achieved incredible things!

Rosalind Franklin

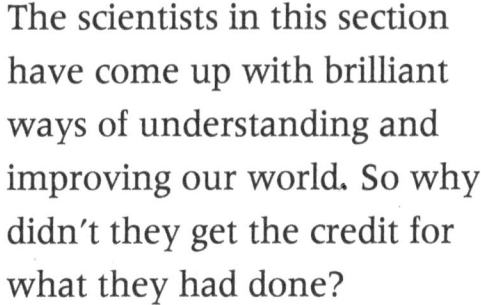

Lise Meitner (1878–1968)

Lise's work changed the world. Along with the scientists Otto Hahn and Otto Frisch, she found a way to **split the atom**.

They believed that splitting the atom would **generate** a huge amount of **energy**. People could then put the energy to good use.

Hero fact

Lise had to leave school when she was 14, but she did not give up on her education. She had to wait until 1901 before she could enrol at university, because women were not allowed to go before then!

Lise and the two Ottos were right! Their discovery is now used to generate electricity.

Otto Hahn got lots of praise and a **Nobel prize**, but Lise did not get the praise she deserved at the time.

Many people felt that Lise should have received a Nobel prize too. That never happened, but in 2010, a university building that was once named after Otto Hahn, was renamed after them both. Better late than never!

HIDDEN HERO AWARD

Lise Meitner

For amazing achievements in science, despite her work being ignored.

Alice Ball (1892–1916)

Alice Ball was an African American scientist. She worked in a time when there was prejudice against both African Americans and women. This makes it even more remarkable that she was so successful.

She studied hard at university, and invented a new way of curing a disease called leprosy – all before she died at the early age of 24.

Hero fact

29th February is Alice Ball Day in Hawaii.

Leprosy is a nasty skin disease. People who caught leprosy were often separated from their families, so that others would not catch the disease.

Alice invented a better way to treat leprosy, using injections. This meant that leprosy patients could return home quickly.

Alice died before she could publish her idea. Instead, one of her **colleagues** renamed Alice's discovery after himself.

Eventually, Alice's work was recognised. The treatment for leprosy is now called the 'Ball method', after Alice.

HIDDEN HERO AWARD

Alice Ball

For amazing discoveries in medicine.

Rosalind Franklin (1920–1958)

Rosalind Franklin was one of the scientists who helped us discover more about DNA.

DNA makes us who we are. It is in all of the cells in our bodies and it affects lots of things – from the colour of our eyes to the types of diseases we might get. DNA is unique to each person.

Hero fact

At the age of 6, Rosalind used to do hard maths sums for fun – and she got them right!

Scientists knew that DNA existed, but they disagreed about what it looked like. Rosalind used X-rays to take a picture of DNA. The picture and her maths calculations helped to answer questions about how DNA worked.

Unfortunately, two **rival** scientists, James Watson and Francis Crick, used Rosalind's data and published their own theory of DNA before Rosalind.

James and Francis got a lot of credit for their theory, but they could not have proved it without Rosalind's data and X-ray picture.

Nowadays, many people believe Rosalind should have shared the credit. This is now being put right. A Rosalind Franklin award is given every year to a woman who has done outstanding scientific work. This is a good way of both remembering Rosalind's achievement and supporting other women in science.

HIDDEN HERO AWARD

Rosalind Franklin

For helping to discover the truth about DNA.

World War wonder women

War often brings out the best – and worst – in people. In this section, we will find out about two people who worked behind the scenes to help defeat Hitler in the Second World War.

Andrée de Jongh

Andrée de Jongh and Joan Clarke saved many lives. It is only now that their stories are being told and they are being given the credit they deserve.

Joan Clarke

The Second World War (1939–1945)

Britain and its allies fought and defeated Germany and its allies. The German leader was called Adolf Hitler.

○ **Andrée de Jongh** (1916–2007)

Andrée was a brave Belgian woman who saved over 400 soldiers' lives by creating The Comet Line. This was an escape route for soldiers who were fighting for Britain and its allies, but were trapped in areas

controlled by German troops. Soldiers used The Comet Line to help them return to Britain, where they could rejoin their **regiments** and go back to fighting the Germans.

Hero fact

The Comet Line stretched over 1200 miles from Belgium to Gibraltar. From there, soldiers and airmen could return to Britain safely.

Andrée and her friends hid the soldiers in attics and cellars. She helped the soldiers disguise themselves, and then led them through France and Spain to safety.

The Comet Line tips

1) No army uniform
2) False papers
3) A good guide

It was a very dangerous journey, and Andrée was nearly captured many times.

In 1943, while helping some troops to safety, Andrée was captured by German soldiers. She was sent to a **concentration camp** for the rest of the war.

Remarkably, The Comet Line continued while Andrée was in the concentration camp. Even more soldiers were rescued.

Without Andrée's work and courage, many more soldiers might have died.

HIDDEN HERO AWARD

Andrée de Jongh

For great bravery and saving many lives during the Second World War.

⚬ Joan Clarke (1917–1996)

Another game changer who helped Britain and its allies win the Second World War was Joan Clarke. She was a mathematician and a code-breaker working in a top-secret government base called Bletchley Park.

The Germans had invented a machine known as the Enigma. It let them send messages in code so that they could keep

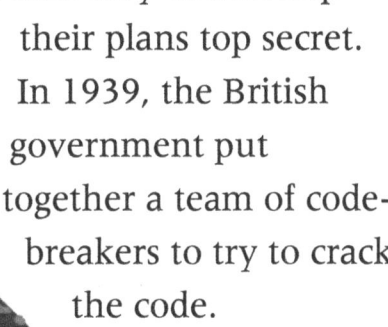

their plans top secret. In 1939, the British government put together a team of code-breakers to try to crack the code.

In 1941, Joan was part of the team who cracked the Enigma code. This meant that Britain could find out where German submarines – called U-boats – were going to be, and then they could avoid them.

Hero fact

At first, Joan was not invited to be part of the code-breaking team because her bosses thought that a woman could not do this sort of work. Soon, however, everyone realised that Joan was just as good as the men.

HIDDEN HERO AWARD

Joan Clarke

For being a star code-breaker and helping to shorten the Second World War.

Incredible inventors

Some inventions change the world with a bang, while other inventions and their inventors are hardly noticed. One of the game-changing inventors in this section created something that you use every day. The other worked on an awesome invention that could be in your home in the future. But neither of these inventors are as well-known as they should be.

Nils Bohlin

Valerie Thomas

It is time to give them the credit they deserve!

Nils Bohlin (1920–2002)

Nils Bohlin invented something that saves lives every single day, and is in every car in the world – the three-point seatbelt.

The seatbelt might not be the most glamorous invention, but it has certainly had a big impact on many people's lives.

Hero fact

Before inventing the three-point seatbelt, Nils designed **ejector seats** for fighter jet planes!

Cars did not always have seatbelts. Even though cars first began to  be popular in about 1908, it was not until nearly fifty years later that most cars had seatbelts. Some were just lap belts and others went across the shoulder, but neither worked perfectly.

 In 1959, Nils invented a way of combining lap belts and shoulder belts to create a belt that was safer than ever.

Hero fact

Seatbelts save around 15,000 lives every year in the USA alone!

Nils's seatbelt was a big success and saved many lives. He was working for Volvo when he invented it, but Volvo later let other car companies use his invention for free.

So next time you get into a car, make sure you buckle up and thank this hidden hero for making your car a safer place to be!

HIDDEN HERO AWARD

Nils Bohlin

For saving over one million lives so far!

Valerie Thomas (1943–)

Valerie Thomas is an African American inventor and scientist.

She first got interested in engineering at the age of eight, when she saw her father trying to mend a broken TV set.

Valerie was keen to learn more and took *The Boys' First Book of Radio and Electronics* out of the library. However, her father did not approve and would not help her with her projects.

Back then, many people thought that electronics was only for boys! At university, Valerie was one of only two women studying electronics.

After university, Valerie got a job at NASA (the American organisation in charge of space science).

Valerie worked on a satellite to send images back from space.

At NASA, she invented the Illusion Transmitter, which can send and receive **three-dimensional** images using mirrors and light.

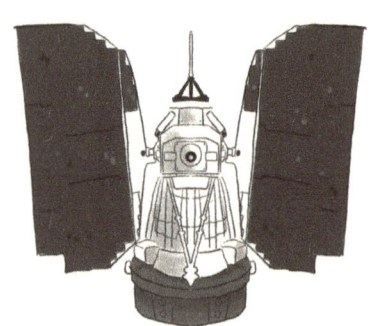

Her invention is used by NASA today and may one day be in your living room instead of your TV!

HIDDEN HERO AWARD

Valerie Thomas

For being a brilliant inventor and holding on to her dream of succeeding in electronics.

Health heroes

Doctors and scientists have come up with inventions and medicines that help us to live longer. People in Britain now live about 25 years longer than they did in 1921!

Let's take a look at three hidden heroes who have helped to improve our health, and give them the recognition they deserve!

Percy Julian

Ignaz Semmelweis   Charles Drew

Ignaz Semmelweis (1818–1865)

The Hungarian doctor Ignaz Semmelweis was laughed at for believing that washing your hands could stop diseases spreading.

Nowadays, hospitals are usually clean and **hygienic**, but hospitals were not always like that. When Ignaz was working in hospitals, doctors did not wash their hands before they treated patients. This meant that patients would sometimes get diseases from their doctors!

Ignaz noticed that many **pregnant** women became ill in hospital, even though they were not sick when they arrived.

Ignaz did some research and discovered that if doctors washed their hands before helping women give birth, it made a big difference because fewer women got sick.

At the time, doctors did not listen. It took years for people to realise that Ignaz was right.

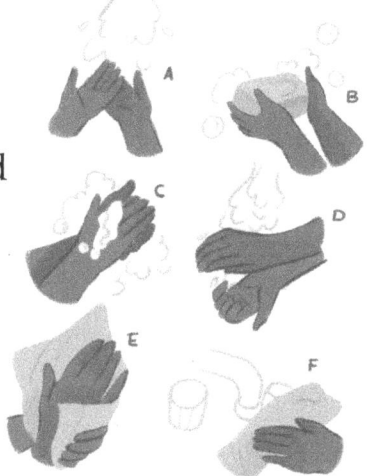

HIDDEN HERO AWARD

Ignaz Semmelweis

For making a simple but life-saving discovery.

Percy Julian (1899–1975)

Percy Julian was an African American scientist. He was not allowed to go to secondary school because there were no local schools  that allowed black students. Despite this, Percy went on to make important medical discoveries.

Percy found a way to make special medicines more cheaply. These special medicines help muscles to grow, and can help with illnesses such as asthma.

Hero fact

Although Percy had not been to secondary school, he was the top pupil in his class at university.

Percy faced difficulties all through his life because he was black. At one point, **racists** set fire to his house – twice!

But Percy did not let **racism** hold him back! In 1961, Percy became one of America's first black millionaires.

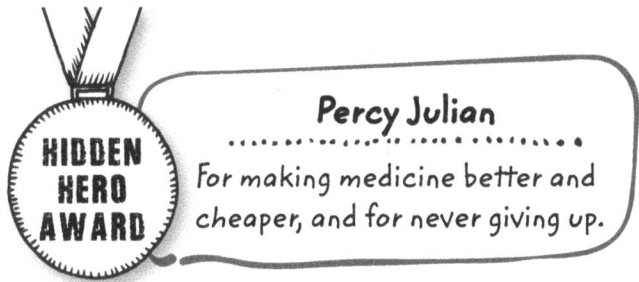

HIDDEN HERO AWARD

Percy Julian
For making medicine better and cheaper, and for never giving up.

Charles Drew (1904–1950)

Charles Drew also faced racism as he tried to make the world a better place.

Sometimes when a person has been injured, they need extra blood to make them better. Charles found a way to dry and store blood in 'blood banks'. Charles's discovery meant that blood lasted longer. It was also easier to transport the blood to where it was needed.

In the Second World War, Charles organised for blood to be sent to Britain to help people who had been injured in the fighting.

In 1941, Charles tried to set up blood banks for American soldiers. He gave up in the end, because the American army wanted black soldiers to only have blood from black people. Charles realised this was racist, but there was nothing he could do. The good thing is that his invention lasted and we still have blood banks today.

HIDDEN HERO AWARD

Charles Drew

For a brilliant invention that helps injured people and saves lives.

Extraordinary explorers

It takes courage to explore new places. Explorers have to be fearless, whether they are climbing high mountains or travelling to distant lands. Gertrude Bell and Tenzing Norgay are two explorers who did amazing things. They were not famous at the time, but now we can put that right!

Gertrude Bell

Tenzing Norgay

⚬ Gertrude Bell (1868–1926)

Gertrude was an explorer, **archaeologist** and spy. She fitted a lot into her life!

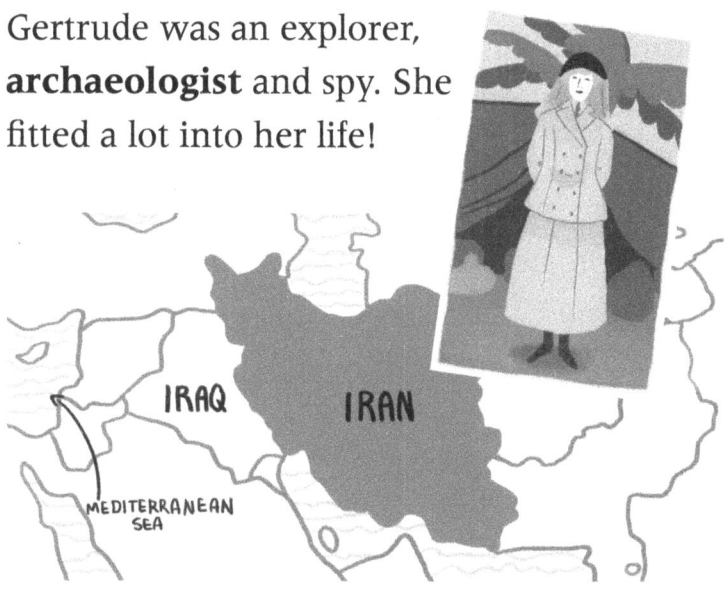

IRAQ

IRAN

MEDITERRANEAN SEA

Gertrude travelled all over the Middle East. She spent a lot of time in the countries we now know as Iran and Iraq. She also fought in the First World War, and discovered and protected many ancient **artefacts**.

Hero fact

Gertrude could speak seven languages!

Gertrude left university in 1892 and went exploring in Persia (which is now the country called Iraq). At that time, many people thought women could not and should not go exploring. Gertrude changed the game by proving that they could. She wrote books and letters about what she learned.

THE LETTERS OF GERTRUDE BELL

When the First World War started in 1914, Gertrude became a spy. Some of the war was fought in the Middle East. She drew maps of the deserts that she had explored. These maps helped British soldiers who were fighting in the area.

Gertrude had adventures in Europe as well as in the Middle East. In 1902, she got caught in a snow storm on a mountain in Switzerland. She survived two days dangling from the end of a rope!

> **Hero fact**
>
> There is a mountain in Switzerland named after Gertrude – Gertrudespitze, which means 'Gertrude's Peak' in German..

Because she was a woman, Gertrude did not get the credit she deserved at the time. Nowadays, more and more people are learning about her – including you!

HIDDEN HERO AWARD

Gertrude Bell
For being a brave adventurer, archaeologist and spy.

Tenzing Norgay (1914–1986)

Tenzing (left) and Edmund (right)

Tenzing Norgay was one of the first two people to reach the top of Mount Everest, the world's highest mountain. The other was Sir Edmund Hillary.

Sir Edmund and Tenzing always refused to say which of them got to the top first. Sir Edmund became famous all over the world, but people thought Tenzing was just his helper. Nowadays, people realise that Tenzing and Edmund were a team, and Tenzing is getting the recognition he deserves.

Tenzing first had the chance to climb Everest when he was twenty years old, and after that, he joined many expeditions to Everest. However, he finally reached the top on 29th May 1953. After that, he always celebrated his birthday on that date because he didn't know when his real birthday was!

Some people feel that Tenzing did not get the same recognition as Sir Edmund because of racism, because he was Asian. However, that is starting to be put right.

In 2015, Tenzing's name went out of this world when scientists named a mountain range on Pluto after him. The Tenzing Montes are icy mountains over two miles high!

The Tenzing Montes on Pluto

HIDDEN HERO AWARD

Tenzing Norgay

For being a brilliant mountaineer and one of the first two people to reach the top of Everest.

Never give up!

We do not always get thanked when we do a good deed or have a brilliant idea. But we can all learn from these hidden heroes. They did not give up when things were difficult, or when people did not appreciate what they had done.

They kept trying, and nowadays they are recognised around the world for the game-changing contributions that they made.

You too could change the world one day. You could make a scientific discovery, or you could create an invention to help save the earth. You could locate a new planet, or you could cure a disease. But you can also help in your own small way, by teaching children to read, volunteering in your local community, or simply by helping someone in need.

Whatever you decide to do, big or small, the most important thing is, never give up!

Glossary

allies	friends or people on the same side
archaeologist	a person who studies objects from the past
artefacts	things made by humans
colleagues	people who work together
concentration camp	a camp where people are kept imprisoned, especially during a war
ejector seat	this helps a pilot to escape from a plane that is about to crash
energy	power that can be used to do things
generate	create or make
hygienic	clean and healthy
Nobel prize	a prize given to people who have done amazing things
pregnant	expecting a baby
racism	being prejudiced against people who have a different skin colour from you
racists	people who are prejudiced against those, or who have a different skin colour from them
regiments	parts of an army

rival	someone who is competing with someone else
split the atom	an atom is the smallest particle of a chemical that can exist. If you split an atom of uranium, it creates a huge amount of energy.
three-dimensional	three-dimensional things have length, breadth and depth (3D)

Index

 # Now answer the questions ...

1 What was Lise Meitner's scientific discovery called?

2 Why were people with leprosy separated from their families? How might they have felt when that happened?

3 What might have happened if Alice Ball hadn't kept going despite the prejudice she faced?

4 How do you think Rosalind Franklin felt when others used her work without giving her credit? How would you feel?

5 What was The Comet Line?

6 What is the meaning of the word 'courage' on page 30?

7 Who do you think was the bravest hidden hero. Why?

8 Which hidden hero do you think made the most amazing contribution?